LITTLE JAMIE BOOK

What It's Like to Be...
Qué se siente al ser...

MARK SÁNCHEZ

BY/POR
KATHLEEN TRACY

TRANSLATED BY/
TRADUCIDO POR
EIDA DE LA VEGA

Mitchell Lane
PUBLISHERS

P.O. Box 196
Hockessin, Delaware 19707
Visit us on the web: www.mitchelllane.com
Comments? email us:
mitchelllane@mitchelllane.com

Mitchell Lane
PUBLISHERS

Printing   1   2   3   4   5   6   7   8   9

A LITTLE JAMIE BOOK

What It's Like to Be . . .   Qué se siente al ser . . .

America Ferrera	América Ferrera
George López	George López
Jennifer López	Jennifer López
The Jonas Brothers	Los Hermanos Jonas
Kaká	Kaká
Mark Sánchez	Mark Sánchez
Marta Vieira	Marta Vieira
Miley Cyrus	Miley Cyrus
Pelé	Pelé
President Barack Obama	El presidente Barack Obama
Ryan Howard	Ryan Howard
Shakira	Shakira
Sonia Sotomayor	Sonia Sotomayor
Vladimir Guerrero	Vladimir Guerrero

Library of Congress Cataloging-in-Publication Data
Tracy, Kathleen.
 What it's like to be Mark Sánchez / by Kathleen Tracy; translated by Eidea de la Vega = ¿Qué se siente al ser Mark Sánchez / por Kathleen Tracy; traducido por Eida de la Vega.
    p. cm. — (A little Jamie book = Un libro little Jaime)
 Includes bibliographical references and index.
 ISBN 978-1-58415-994-0 (library bound)
1. Sánchez, Mark—Juvenile literature. 2. Football players—United States—Biography—Juvenile literature. 3. Quarterbacks (Football—United States—Biography—Juvenile literature. 4. Hispanic American football players—Biography—Juvenile literature. I. Vega, Eida de la. II. Title. III. Title: ¿Qué se siente al ser el Mark Sánchez.
 GV939.S175T73 2011
 796.332092—dc22
 [B]
                                                                          2011006179

PLB

What It's Like to Be... /
Qué se siente al ser...
MARK
SÁNCHEZ

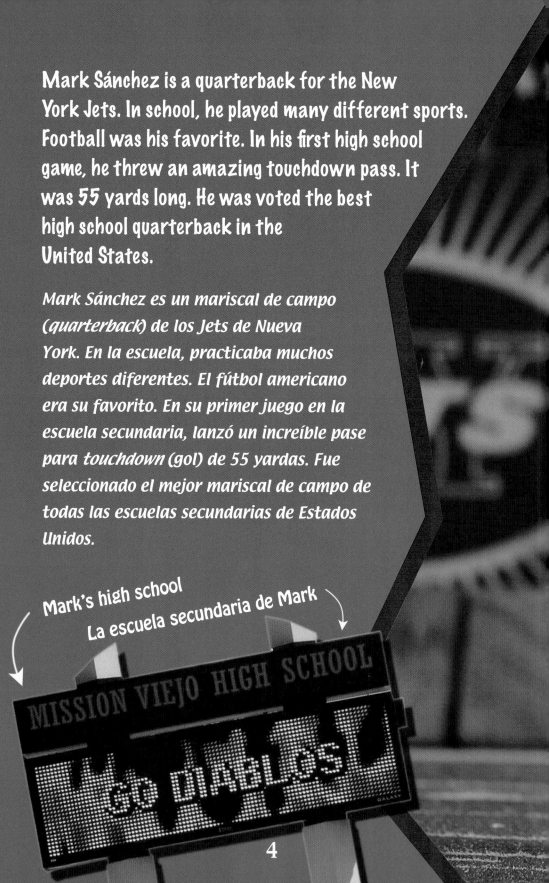

Mark Sánchez is a quarterback for the New York Jets. In school, he played many different sports. Football was his favorite. In his first high school game, he threw an amazing touchdown pass. It was 55 yards long. He was voted the best high school quarterback in the United States.

Mark Sánchez es un mariscal de campo (quarterback) de los Jets de Nueva York. En la escuela, practicaba muchos deportes diferentes. El fútbol americano era su favorito. En su primer juego en la escuela secundaria, lanzó un increíble pase para *touchdown* (gol) de 55 yardas. Fue seleccionado el mejor mariscal de campo de todas las escuelas secundarias de Estados Unidos.

Mark's high school
La escuela secundaria de Mark

MISSION VIEJO HIGH SCHOOL

GO DIABLOS

MARK SÁNCHEZ

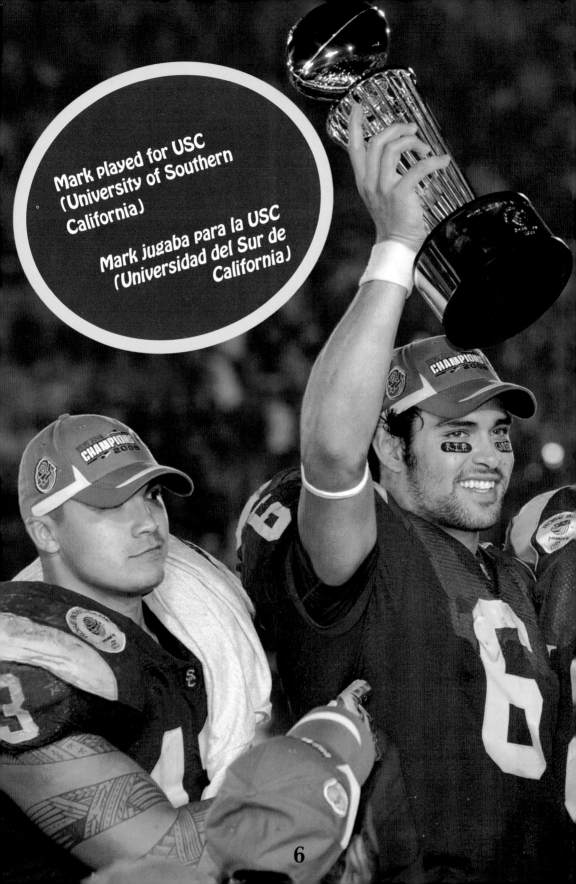

Mark played for USC
(University of Southern
California)

Mark jugaba para la USC
(Universidad del Sur de
California)

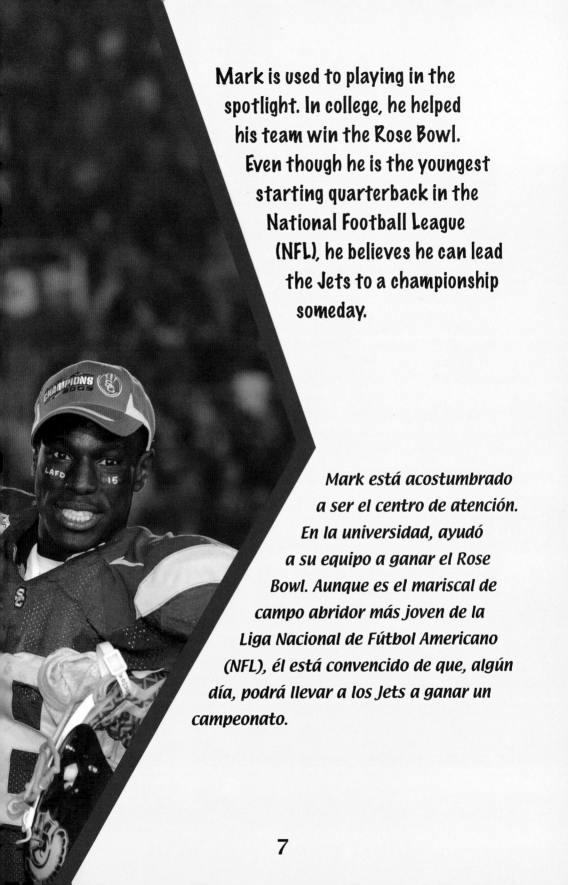

Mark is used to playing in the spotlight. In college, he helped his team win the Rose Bowl. Even though he is the youngest starting quarterback in the National Football League (NFL), he believes he can lead the Jets to a championship someday.

Mark está acostumbrado a ser el centro de atención. En la universidad, ayudó a su equipo a ganar el Rose Bowl. Aunque es el mariscal de campo abridor más joven de la Liga Nacional de Fútbol Americano (NFL), él está convencido de que, algún día, podrá llevar a los Jets a ganar un campeonato.

7

Mark was born on November 11, 1986. His great-grandparents were from Mexico. He and his older brothers, Nick Jr. and Brandon, grew up in California. Their father, Nick Sr., told each of them that their brothers were "going to be your best friends." Now Mark and Brandon live together in New Jersey. Their home is close to the Jets training center.

Mark nació el 11 de noviembre de 1986. Sus bisabuelos eran de México. Mark y sus hermanos mayores, Nick y Brandon, crecieron en California. Su padre, que también se llama Nick, les dijo a cada uno que sus hermanos "van a ser tus mejores amigos". Ahora Mark y Brandon viven juntos en Nueva Jersey. Su casa está cerca del centro de entrenamiento de los Jets.

8

DAD
(PAPÁ)

SANC

Jets training center in Florham Park, New Jersey

Centro de entrenamiento de los Jets en Florham Park, Nueva Jersey

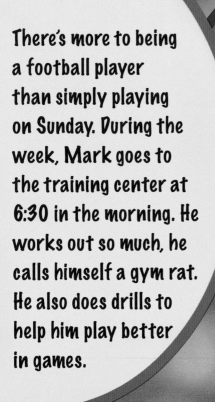

There's more to being a football player than simply playing on Sunday. During the week, Mark goes to the training center at 6:30 in the morning. He works out so much, he calls himself a gym rat. He also does drills to help him play better in games.

Un jugador de fútbol americano no sólo tiene que jugar los domingos. Durante la semana, Mark va al centro de entrenamiento a las 6:30 de la mañana. Hace tanto ejercicio, que él mismo se llama ratón de gimnasio. También hace prácticas que lo ayudan a jugar mejor los partidos.

Mark tests a new video game with teammate Nick Mangold.

Mark prueba un nuevo videojuego con su compañero de equipo, Nick Mangold.

On game day, Mark gets to the stadium early. After he warms up, he relaxes by listening to pop music on his iPod. He enjoys Elton John, Billy Joel, and the Dave Matthews Band.

Right before the game starts, Mark and his teammates run out onto the field. They stand on the sideline and sing "The Star-Spangled Banner."

SIR ELTON JOHN

Cuando hay partidos, Mark llega al estadio temprano.
Después de hacer ejercicios de calentamiento, se relaja
escuchando música pop en su iPod. Le gustan Elton John,
Billy Joel y la banda de Dave Matthews.

Antes de que empiece el partido, Mark y sus compañeros
salen corriendo al campo. Se paran en las líneas
laterales y cantan el himno de Estados Unidos, "La
bandera de estrellas centelleantes".

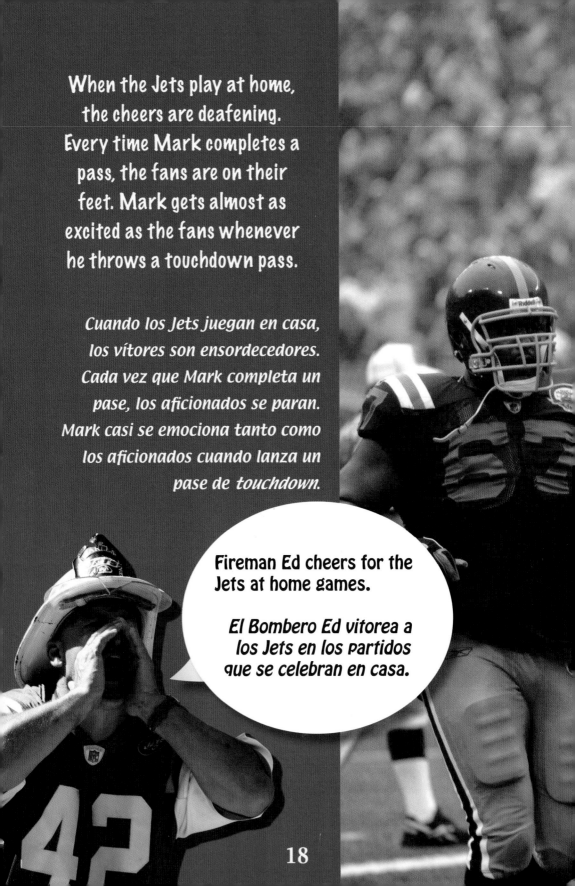

When the Jets play at home, the cheers are deafening. Every time Mark completes a pass, the fans are on their feet. Mark gets almost as excited as the fans whenever he throws a touchdown pass.

Cuando los Jets juegan en casa, los vítores son ensordecedores. Cada vez que Mark completa un pase, los aficionados se paran. Mark casi se emociona tanto como los aficionados cuando lanza un pase de touchdown.

Fireman Ed cheers for the Jets at home games.

El Bombero Ed vitorea a los Jets en los partidos que se celebran en casa.

Mark (6) was the first rookie quarterback in Jets history to start on opening day.

Mark (6) fue el primer mariscal de campo novato en la historia de los Jets al que le permitieron abrir el juego en el primer partido de la temporada.

19

Tony Award
Premio Tony

Mark gets invited to a lot of events, such as the Tony Awards for live theater. He became a theater fan when he moved to New York. His teammates tease him because he likes Broadway musicals, but he doesn't let that change his mind.

A Mark lo invitan a montones de eventos, tales como los Premios Tony de teatro. Se aficionó al teatro cuando se mudó a Nueva York. Sus compañeros de equipo se burlan de él porque le gustan los musicales de Broadway, pero él no deja que eso le haga cambiar de idea.

D'BRICKASHAW FERGUSON

He and teammate D'Brickashaw Ferguson attended a state dinner with U.S. President Barack Obama. The White House dinner was in honor of Mexican President Felipe Calderón.

Él y su compañero de equipo, D'Brickashaw Ferguson, asistieron a una cena de estado con el presidente de Estados Unidos, Barack Obama. La cena en la Casa Blanca fue en honor del presidente mexicano Felipe Calderón.

Mexican President
Calderón

U.S. President
Obama

*El presidente
mexicano Calderón*

*El presidente de
EE. UU. Obama*

23

24

Whenever Mark goes out, he will take time to sign autographs for Jets fans. He also enjoys meeting fans after the games.

Siempre que Mark sale, dedica tiempo a firmarles autógrafos a los admiradores de los Jets. También disfruta reunirse con ellos después de los partidos.

ROOKIE

COLLECTION

THREADS

MARK SANCHEZ
JETS

As a role model for Hispanic youth, he learned how to speak Spanish. He no longer needs a translator to talk to Spanish-speaking fans.

Como ejemplo para la juventud hispana, aprendió a hablar español. Ya no necesita traductor para hablar con sus admiradores hispanohablantes.

Mark uses his fame to help others. He works for many charities both in New York and in California. He believes it is important to help others. He doesn't want to forget how lucky he is to be successful.

Mark usa su fama para ayudar a otros. Trabaja para muchas beneficencias tanto en Nueva York como en California. Cree que es importante ayudar a otros. No quiere olvidar lo afortunado que es por haber

INNER-CITY GAMES
LOS ANGELES

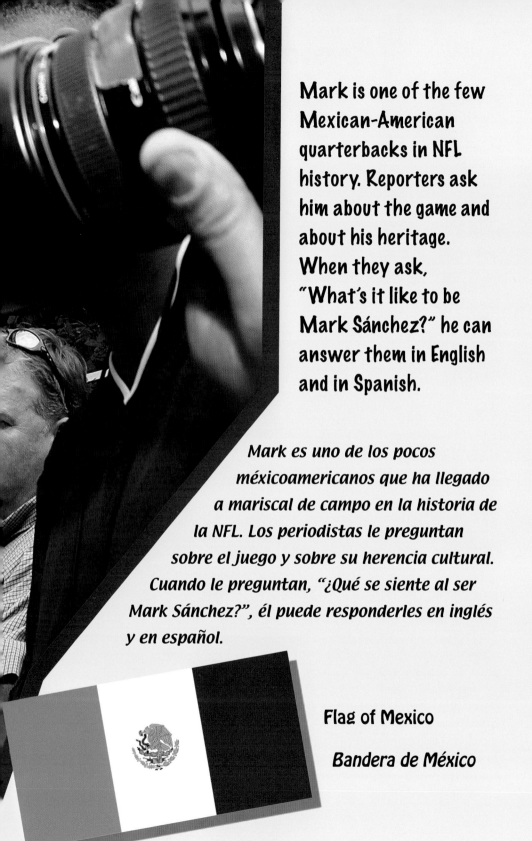

Mark is one of the few Mexican-American quarterbacks in NFL history. Reporters ask him about the game and about his heritage. When they ask, "What's it like to be Mark Sánchez?" he can answer them in English and in Spanish.

Mark es uno de los pocos méxicoamericanos que ha llegado a mariscal de campo en la historia de la NFL. Los periodistas le preguntan sobre el juego y sobre su herencia cultural. Cuando le preguntan, "¿Qué se siente al ser Mark Sánchez?", él puede responderles en inglés y en español.

Flag of Mexico

Bandera de México

GLOSSARY

autograph (AW-toh-graf) — To sign one's name on something.

championship (CHAM-pee-un-ship) — A game between the best two teams; the winner of this game is declared the champion.

charity (CHAY-rih-tee) — A group that raises money to help people in need.

chorizo (chuh-REE-zoh) — A spicy sausage made with pork, chili peppers, and garlic.

drill — An exercise that is repeated in order to improve a skill.

heritage (HAYR-ih-tij) — The cultural history of one's family.

quarterback (KWAR-ter-bak) — The football player who directs the plays and throws the passes.

rookie (ROO-kee) — Someone in his or her first year on a job.

Rose Bowl — The most important championship game between college football teams.

touchdown pass (TUTCH-down PAS) — A throw to a player who scores a touchdown.

translator (TRANS-lay-tor) — Someone who helps people who speak different languages communicate.

GLOSARIO

autógrafo — firmar tu nombre sobre algo

beneficencia — un grupo que recoge dinero para ayudar a personas necesitadas

campeonato — un partido entre los dos mejores equipos; el ganador de este partido se declara campeón

chorizo — una salchicha de cerdo, pimiento y ajo

herencia cultural — la tradición cultural de una familia

mariscal de campo — el jugador de fútbol americano que dirige las jugadas y lanza los pases

novato — alguien en su primer año en un trabajo

pase de *touchdown* — un lanzamiento a un jugador que marca un *touchdown* o gol

práctica — un ejercicio que se repite para mejorar una destreza

Rose Bowl — el partido más importante entre los equipos universitarios de fútbol americano

touchdown — la forma básica de anotar en el fútbol americano

traductor — alguien que ayuda a comunicarse a personas que hablan idiomas diferentes

FURTHER READING/LECTURAS RECOMENDADAS

Works Consulted/Obras consultadas

Arangure, Jorge, Jr. "*¡Viva Sánchez!*" *ESPN The Magazine*, August 11, 2008. http://sports.espn.go.com/espnmag/story?id=3511275

Cimini, Rich. "Jet's Message Board." *Daily News*, September 5, 2009. http://forums.theganggreen.com/showthread.php?t=47920

Lev, Michael. "NFL Draft: The Mark Sanchez Interview." *Orange County Register*, February 13, 2009. http://usc.ocregister.com/2009/02/13/nfl-draft-the-mark-sanchez-interview-part-3-of-3/10275/

McNeal, Wendy. "Mark Sanchez Scores a Touchdown with Kids." *NBC Los Angeles*, May 11, 2010. http://www.nbclosangeles.com/news/sports/Mark-Sanchez-Scores-a-Touchdown-With-Kids-93444704.html.

Mehta, Manish. "Mark Sanchez Knows He Must Improve Accuracy after Watching Film of Jets' 9-0 Loss to Packers." *New York Daily News*, November 4, 2010. http://www.nydailynews.com/sports/football/jets/2010/11/04/2010-11-04_sanchez_aims_to_be_on_target.html#ixzz15x6QySqE

Books

Williams, Zella. *Mark Sánchez: Quarterback on the Rise*. New York: PowerKids Press, 2010.

Libros

Taylor, Trace y Sánchez, Lucía. *Fútbol americano (Deportes)*. King of Prussia, PA: ARC Press, 2010.

Williams, Zella. *Mark Sánchez: Mariscal de campo en ascenso*. New York: Editorial Buenas Letras, 2010.

On the Internet

Mark Sanchez, New York Jets NFL http://www.nfl.com/players/marksanchez/profile?id=SAN091667

Mark Sanchez Profile, New York Jets, ESPN.com http://sports.espn.go.com/nfl/players/profile?playerId=12482

Official Site of the New York Jets http://www.newyorkjets.com/

En Internet

"Mark Sánchez" http://es.wikipedia.org/wiki/Mark_Sanchez

Sitio Oficial de los Jets de Nueva York http://www.newyorkjets.com/espanol/index.html

COVER DESIGN: Joe Rasemas
PHOTO CREDITS: Cover (left), pp. 3, 20-21—Dimitrios Kambouris/WireImage; cover (right), p. 5—AP Photo/Evan Pinkus; pp. 6–7—AP Photo/Mark J. Terrill; pp. 8–9—AP Photo/Rich Schultz; pp. 10–11—Ronald C. Modra/Sports Imagery/Getty Images; pp. 12-13, 16-17, 24-25, 28-29—Al Pereira/Getty Images; pp. 14–15—James Devaney/WireImage/Getty Images; p. 15—Mike Coppola/Getty Images for XBOX; pp. 18–19—Andrew Theodorakis/NY Daily News Archive via Getty Images; pp. 22–23— TIM SLOAN/AFP/Getty Images; p. 26—Jim Rogash/Getty Images. All other photos—CreativeCommons. Every effort has been made to locate all copyright holders of materials used in this book. Any errors or omissions will be corrected in future editions of the book.

INDEX/ÍNDICE

Calderón, Felipe 22, 23
chorizo 11
fans / aficionados 18, 25, 27
Ferguson, D'Brickashaw 22
Fireman Ed / Bombero Ed 18
game day / día del partido 16–17, 18
Mangold, Nick 15
Mexico / México 8, 22, 23, 29
New York Jets / Jets de Nueva York 4, 7, 8, 9,
Obama, Barack 22, 23
rookie / novato 19
Rose Bowl 7
Sánchez, Brandon (brother / hermano) 8, 14
Sánchez, Mark
  awards and honors / premios y honores 4, 19, 22
  charity work / labor de beneficencia 27

family / familia 8, 9, 14
heritage / herencia 8, 27, 29
hobbies / pasatiempos 4, 14, 16–17, 21
music / música 16–17, 21
school / escuela 4
training / entrenamiento 8, 9, 10, 13
Sánchez, Nick, Jr. (brother / hermano) 8
"The Star-Spangled Banner" / "La bandera de estrellas centelleantes" 16–17
Tony Awards / Premios Tony 21
touchdown pass / pase para touchdown 4, 18
University of Southern California / Universidad del Sur de California 6, 7

ABOUT THE AUTHOR: Entertainment journalist and children's book author Kathleen Tracy specializes in celebrity biographies. An avid sports fan, she lives in Southern California with her two dogs and African Grey parrot.

ACERCA DE LA AUTORA: La periodista y escritora de libros para niños, Kathleen Tracy, se especializa en biografías de personas famosas. Kathleen es muy aficionada a los deportes y vive en el sur de California con sus dos perros y un loro gris africano.

ABOUT THE TRANSLATOR: Eida de la Vega was born in Havana, Cuba, and now lives in New Jersey with her mother, her husband, and her two children. Eida has worked at Lectorum/Scholastic, and as editor of the magazine *Selecciones del Reader's Digest*.

ACERCA DE LA TRADUCTORA: Eida de la Vega nació en La Habana, Cuba, y ahora vive en Nueva Jersey con su madre, su esposo y sus dos hijos. Ha trabajado en Lectorum/Scholastic y, como editora, en la revista *Selecciones del Reader's Digest*.